How to Be Positive
In 30 Days
S. Kluiter

Nothing Last Forever-
Things change. This is important to remember. The situation you are in now will not be the same situation that you will be in five years from now. When you are down it is hard to see tomorrow. When your grand plan falls short or completely fails finding the good that awaits you in the future is often times your most difficult task. If you make good positive choices now you can have a good positive future.

A main point in Buddhism is that life is suffering. It is to acknowledge that bad things will happen. There will be hardships. You will not have a glorious great day every day. However knowing this we are able to accept that things are or can be difficult and that bad things do happen and we can perceiver.

Using this book you will be able to direct your life with positive momentum. You will fall from grace. You will become negative again. It's an easy slip. But using what you learn here you will rise above that fall and achieve the future you deserve.

Preface-
If you picked up this book you're in luck. There is a cure for your ailment and it's you. You are the only one who can control your mind. The number one defining thing of successful individuals is positivity. Every successful person in this world has a positive outlook on life. There mountains of books about it. Nearly every self help book you read will tell you to remain positive. It's a fact so important to success that nearly every business book about being a successful business owner mentions it repeatedly. Being positive is the core concept behind living a good life.

A common misconception is that happiness comes from being healthy and successful. In truth it is the opposite. It all starts in your mind. It is easier to be negative than positive. Negativity is a hard road to come back from. Your brain is likely trained to tell you when you can't do things or that you don't deserve things. Thankfully you can train your brain like any other muscle to exert positive thoughts opposed to negative responses. It will take time and it will take energy but it will be worth it in the end. After 30 days you will feel like a different person. Not someone changed at the core or of a different moral compass, but an individual whose brain has been trained to exert positive thoughts to yield positive outcomes.

There is a popular theory called the law of attraction. In this theory the basic idea is that if you envision yourself having achieved a goal you will attract achieving that goal. Because you've already mentally won you only have to physically take action. Positive thoughts attract positive results. If you believe that you can obtain a promotion or run a marathon and believe can imagine that you already have you are more likely to complete your goal.

Why write this?

Because I used to be a negative person. I was raised in a household of can't. I was in a relationship with a person who believed that they didn't have the skills and abilities to succeed. I was depressed and in a downward spiral of failure. By changing my mindset i corrected my life path. From a dead end job to a career and a home with nice things. All though the power of positive thinking. And it's amazing because positivity is just as contagious as negativity. The seeds are just harder to grow. We are all standing on a hill. The vertical climb is steep and rough but has rewards. It's where positivity lives. The gentle slope downward is where your mind lays the seeds of negativity. A place that's easy to fall to. A place to which we generally invite our friends and family to join us in.

This is a system that I used to train my brain. After completing the system you will hear things from coworkers and family members that might make you feel different. That's ok. These may include but are not limited to:

"What make you think you can achieve that?"

"I could never do that."

"You can't do that." (Because they are negative.)

"I don't know how you remain so positive."

"I wish I thought like you."

"Why are you so positive all the time? It's annoying!" (When they can't get over their own negativity.)

"How can today be a good day when (insert event)."

"You're stupid if you think everything is going to work out good! I live in the real world"

"I'm not going to lie to myself and say that things are good when they aren't."

"I'm not dumb enough to lie to myself about my abilities."

"I'm not like you. I can't just do things."

People who say things like this are two be treated in one of two ways. Firstly and preferably you can help them by offering an alternative perspective on their outlook on life. Secondly, you can distance yourself from their tainted attitude.

To start I recommend by distancing yourself from the negative people in your life. This will make your path to positivity easier. Seek out people who are positive and successful. We become our surroundings. If you are not sure where to meet people who are positive try joining meetup groups from MeetUp.com. The people at these events are generally happy social people who want to help each other succeed or share a specialized common interest.

To get the most out of this book you may have to read it multiple times. And yes some of it might seem repetitive. Carry it with you in your phone. Look through it when you need a pick me up. Read quotes when you need them. After 30 days of practicing what is taught in this book you will be more positive.

Your body-

Your body is an extension of your mind and your is the leader of your body. What you think your body will do. As your body experiences the world it is expressing the thoughts present in your mind. If you are happy you walk with more pep in your step. You have a longer stride. Your arms swing more and you have a smile. The body radiates your emotions. That's how we know when each other are angry or sad.

If you stand in a powerful stance you will find that you feel more powerful. To do so stand with your feet aligned with your shoulders and your hands at your hips. This stance is associated with power in our minds so we feel more powerful when we take it. A wide body spread out taking up space is a show of power. The same works for if you ball yourself up into a position where you take up less space. You feel more confined as though you have lost or are less powerful.

The same is true with emotions. You've heard the saying "fake it until you make it". It's not just some stupid line in a movie or a joke between friends. It is a truth that you can use to your advantage. If you act happy and walk with a happy cheerful stride you will experience a change of emotion. You will feel happier because your mind associates your bodies movements with happiness. Amy Cuddy talks about this in her Ted Talk from Ted Global 2012 where he states that walking in a happy way with swinging arms and happy wide moments improves happiness.

It's all the associations you build inside your own mind.

A study published by the Journal of *Psychological Science* in 2011 found that people who stood or sat in expansive poses for just one minute not only had feelings of being more powerful and in charge but it affected their mind and body so much so that they had an increase testosterone and a decrease in the stress hormone cortisol.

What does this have to do with creating a positive mental attitude?

Everything. Can you control your physical behavior? Yes. Does your physical behavior alter your mental state and emotions? Yes. By feeling happier and more powerful we can begin to get our minds used to being positive. Positioning your body in ways of power will help you to do so. No one enjoys feeling powerless. Promoting happiness will help you become more positive. It is in the building of small habits that we can reprogram our minds and bodies towards a positive outlook.

Exercise

I'm fat. I should probably weigh at least 50 lbs less than what I do. So if you've seen pictures of me you might wonder where I get off telling you that exercise is essential. Well it is. I might not run a mile a day or bench 200 but that's not what matters. What matters is that you get your blood moving. I don't care if it's a walk in the morning meant to clear your head or yoga to loosen you up.

This is exercise not just for physical health but mental as well. When you sit and do nothing and wallow in your thoughts it is easy to fall to negativity. But when you get up and moving and achieve something that gets your blood pumping it will set you on a path towards positivity.

Reading

    I can't express the need to read. If not daily than weekly. If you feel that you are straying down the path negativity reread sections of this book or pick up other books that will be mentioned within the chapters and in the back of the book. I included this list of readings that I personally recommend not only for maintaining positivity but also learning about success in general. This list has not been included as a part of a promotion from a publishing studio. They are are included because these are the books that I know for a fact helped me and others like me.

Meditation

Meditation can be used to clear your mind. Meditation has effects on the body and the mind. It's soothing effects have even been shown in increase testosterone production in men. I personally do not practice daily meditation but I have friends who have and found it very helpful in maintaining their mental state.

Do you like selfies?

Good. Studies show people who take selfies are happier. Probably because of the positive reinforcement of likes on social media. If you don't typically take selfies. Try it, it might cheer you up.

What you should do every day

When someone says something negative you say something positive. Not in your head. Not quietly under your breath. Outwardly to them.

As example, "Today sucks! We are short staffed."

"But we can still get it done and if we work late we will get overtime." Or "It only sucks if you let it. We have a good team. We can probably get it done in the same amount of time."

You have to fight for positivity.

A reinforcing reason to keep on top of keeping positive-

"When you feel good about yourself you get more done." - The One Minute Manager That's why it's important to not only keep yourself positive so you feel good but to give positivity to those around you.

There's a reason motivational posters are so popular.

There's a reason nearly all of us like them. They enforce something we want to believe whether we act on that belief or not we desire it. Many of these are based on the idea of remaining positive or climbing mountains. Overcoming adversity. Metaphors of how to live life or be a better person. The person we want to be, nay, the person we long to be. Surround yourself with things that bring out the positive side of you.

Learning and habit formation

You will see that humans learn best from repetition. That habits are formed from consistent repetition. So occasionally I will repeat myself and I will ask you to repeat yourself. Not because I think you are stupid or cannot understand something when you read it once. But because it will enforce you learning better. Because the major part of this book is changing your mental habits within 30 days. To do so we will not only with repetition but by challenging your thought habits and reactions to circumstances. If I can learn by reading this way and science backs these methods for learning than you too can learn in this way.

People can feel positivity in email and texts too

People can tell if you are positive and negative in every form of communication and vice versa. Keep this in mind when associating with negative individuals and positive individuals. As well as for how you are communicating with others.

It can be a helpful check to pause and read through what you are about to send to others in text or email and gage your positivity or negativity. This will ensure that you are not slipping from your positive mind set.

On complaints.
"Complainers drain energy. If you associate with people who complain you will become more complacent. If you complain you will drink you energy and the energy of those around you. Complains ruin attitude." - How to Get to the Top by Jeffrey J. Fox

Catch yourself complaining. This will take time. This will take training. You will think of a complaint and move to voice it. STOP. Put your complaints aside. Put the complaints of others aside and move forward.

On Weather
Don't get upset about the weather. You can't change it. You can't control it. The fact that you got rained on will not affect you for more than about 15 minutes and that's just because you're waiting for your shirt to dry. The

weather did not ruin your day unless you allowed it to. Find a solution.

You Become Your Surroundings

Are your friends negative? Are your coworkers negative? Is your spouse negative? Distance yourself from negativity. You take on the attributes of the company you keep. That being said and it being established that others affect us we know that we can effect others. By being positive and maintaining positivity outwardly you can positively affect the lives of those you care about.

Positivity in the Workplace

It can be difficult to keep positive at work. Between deadlines and quotas. Especially if you work a position that is high stress. The best way to combat this is to view your work as your own business. Take ownership for what you do. Act as you would if you were the owner and one day you might be. If your money were being put into this workplace how would you act?

Being positive will move you forward in your career. Two people stand out in a workplace. The overall positive and the negative.

Reinforce your positivity with the words of others

Reading a quote from someone positive you admire like Tony Robbins, W. Clement Stone, or Napoleon Hill can help to reinforce your positive mind set. Every other page of this book has a quote about positivity to reinforce and uplift that mindset within you.

The Cause of All Your Problems

What is the cause of all of your problems? If the chair wasn't blue I could have sold more chairs. If the dog hadn't gotten sick I'd have been able to spend the weekend on the lake! What are you blaming? Take a moment and list all the things causing you problems and holding you back. Complete this before turning the page.

All your problems continued
What is the top of your list? Is it you?

This books is about changing the way you think. Blaming others or events for your problems or hardships is a path to negative thought. Purge all negative thought. Take two more seconds and put your name at the top of your list. You are your only problem and you are also your only solution. You are all that holds you back. Accept this and move on.

Being positive is easier if you do not place blame on others. Do not focus on blame. Today keep your mind open and be alert for yourself and others placing blame. Find solutions not blame. Solutions are better.

When you blame you breed negativity. When you find a solution you solve a problem and solving problems stimulates your brain in a positive way.

This is a practice in redirecting your thoughts and emotions. Training you to push positive after being negative.

Always remember it's easier to blame others than to accept that you yourself could ever be at fault for your situation. The harder road has less regret.

Misery Loves Company.
Positivity loves Company too.

Positive

When I worked at Combined Insurance one thing that we constantly enforced was the importance of a positive mental attitude. Positive Mental Attitude was consistently enforced. The company developed a cheer that was part of every meeting we had and as a part of it was Positive Mental Attitude. After leaving the company I still saw a use for this and grew to develop my own saying which I repeat to myself every day. You should too. Start your day and if you have team meetings start your team meeting with something about positivity.

Every morning I tell myself "It's going to be the best day ever."

If the sky is falling and my car won't stop, it's going to be the best day ever. Even if it starts as a joke I keep saying it to myself and to others. When you tell a coworker it's going to be the best day ever you will get a few odd responses. Some might even argue with you. Some might think that you're crazy. I've experienced them both.

But then I saw a change. (I was working in the kitchen of a nursing home at the time and didn't even realize what I was doing). Not only a change in myself but in my coworkers. I was working with negative people for nine hours a day. It's hard to be positive in an environment that encourages negativity. So I was captain positive. It was like a joke, even to myself for the first few weeks. We would be short staffed and I would say it's going to be the best day ever! We would have 10 problems and 4 upset customers. It's going to be the best day ever. And they'd roll their eyes at me. And then there would be a smile. A small smile. Then it became a joke and my coworkers started to smile and jokingly say it to each other. Perhaps they were mocking me. It didn't matter. A joke turned into a reality. Soon our crew was having fun at work! It took a little over two months to see the full change. Sure people got negative every now and again. It was their habit. But not at work. Not with me. With me our team could do anything. My positivity expressed outwardly turned me into an emotional leader which turned us into a positive team.

Develop your own saying or borrow mine. This saying isn't just to keep an idea of something positive in your mind, it's to project it outwardly. Take your positivity slogan and write it down. When I first started I wrote It's going to be the best day ever on sticky notes and placed one at my computer so I saw it while working, one on my wall so it was the first thing I saw when I woke up, and in two locations in my car so I would read it and be reminded while traveling to prevent my mind from wandering.

Reinforce the thought.

Take Day one to find out where you need to be reminded to be positive. Maybe you need to change the background on your phone. Maybe you need a reminder on your calendar so you get an alert 1-3 times a day. I've done both of them as well. They work.

At the end of your day take a moment to look back and examine your day. Reflect on your moments of negativity and figure out how you could have handled them more positively. This should only take a couple of minutes. Then look at how positive you were the rest of your day and congratulate yourself.

Lastly, now that you're thinking about positivity throughout the day, who are the negative people in your life? Remember that it is important not to blame them or think ill of them for their thoughts or negativity. However it is important to recognize where negativity comes from so that you can distance yourself from it or be prepared to confront it.

Repetition-

Practice makes perfect, as the saying goes.

I honestly used to wake up everyday and my first thought would be that I wanted to die. I'd think it throughout the day. I didn't know what I was doing or why I was doing it. I was just kind of living and allowing my negative mindset to drag me further and further into despair.

I'd built up a habit. I'd built up triggers into my mindset. When I woke up I had a thought. So I knew that if my brain could be wired to have a negative thought at the start of my day than I could train it to have a positive one. This took some time. Remembering to force good positive affirmations seconds after waking was a struggle. It took weeks of focusing on it and have it actually show up as a pop up alert on my phone (which I used as my alarm) so I could read it to bring positive thoughts in. Every day I woke up to, "It's gunna be the best day ever." until when I woke up that was my first thought.

Repetition. Muscle memory. Positive reinforcement. Getting into a habit of pushing positive thoughts while getting ready in the morning opposed to thinking about everything I had to do that day. Building the foundation of my day. Laying brick after brick until building those bricks became habit. Until I didn't have to make myself think positive. I was positive.

Counter arguing with yourself-

You have to counter your own thoughts. We all have thoughts that lean negative. It's not ok. Were not going to accept that any more. You need to be comfortable confronting yourself and calling yourself out on your own behavior. It's harder to catch yourself than it is to catch a friend or family member. We often times don't realize when we are becoming negative. It's not a light on or light off mind set. It's a slow downward slope. Almost as gentle as the curve of the Earth. You can hardly see it until you get far enough away to see that the land is not flat but a sphere.

Take a moment once a day and zoom out from yourself and ask, where is my mindset? What trajectory am I on? Do I like where my thoughts are headed?

If you're moving towards negativity take a second to identify the little thoughts that are popping up in your mind and create counter arguments.

"I don't have skills to do this job!" I can learn the skills to do this job!

"I could never do what he/she did!" If they did it I could do it too!

"I'm a shitty person and everyone hates me!" Why do people hate you? Why would people hate you? (I assure you there are very few people in this world who are actually hated or disliked by large amounts of people)

Once you sit down and look at reasoning behind your negative thoughts and try to answer why you would think them there's generally not a good answer. Negativity isn't logical.

Self Check 1

What is your saying and have you said it to yourself today?

Where is your mindset? How do you feel?

Good. Great. Fantastic. Wonderful.

Self Check 2

How you see the world is determined by your mindset.

Is today going to be a good day?

Have you seen an adjustment in your attitude in the days since starting your path towards change?

Remember change takes time. Do not be discouraged if you haven't seen results yet.

We are in the process of breaking a pattern. Your brain may have been wired to think negative thoughts. To push back your outward thoughts. Stay strong. It takes time to write a computer program. It takes time to rewire your brain. It takes time for others to adjust to your change.

Stress brings us down. It makes it easier to be negative. Stress is enemy number one. Stress needs to be managed. Exercise can help with stress. Meditation can help with stress. A positive outlook can help with stress. Stress holds down negative thoughts.

Practice positivity today and look for ways to reduce stress in your life. What are the major stressors in your life? Are bills piling up? Is work overwhelming? Is it raining and your shoes are wet causing you to have to squish your way step by step around the office? Sounds annoying. But it's not a problem. Can you fix your bills? Yes. It may take time but no situation is permanent.

It is important to be optimistic. Optimism will crush negative thoughts before you have them. Respond to every situation with a best case scenario view.

Self Check 3

Are the people you spend the majority of your time with positive or negative?

If you answered negative it's time to help them or distance yourself from their negativity.

Conclusion

You will not see an immediate change in our attitude from reading this. Change takes time. Use what you have learned and within 30 days you will see positive change. Just like I have.

Book Recommendations-
- Think and Grow Rich - Napoleon Hill
- Success Through a Positive Mental Attitude - W. Clement Stone
- The Greatest Salesman in the World - Og Mandino
- The Power of Positive Thinking by Norman Vincent Peale
- How to Win Friends and Influence People by Dale Carnegie
- As a Man Thinketh by James Allen
- Awaken The Giant Within – Anthony Robbins

www.ingramcontent.com/pod-product-compliance
Lightning Source LLC
Chambersburg PA
CBHW031517210526
45464CB00007B/2959